LOOP

BOOKS BY ANNE SIMPSON

POETRY
Light Falls Through You (2000)
Loop (2003)

FICTION
Canterbury Beach (2001)

LOOP

ANNE SIMPSON

M&S

National Library of Canada Cataloguing in Publication

Simpson, Anne, 1956–
Loop / Anne Simpson.

Poems.
ISBN 0-7710-8075-1

I. Title.

PS8587.I54533L66 2003   C811'.6   C2002-905226-2
PR9199.3.S527L66 2003

We acknowledge the financial support of the Government of Canada through the Book Publishing Industry Development Program for our publishing activities. We further acknowledge the support of the Canada Council for the Arts and the Ontario Arts Council for our publishing program.

Typeset in Centaur by M&S, Toronto
Printed and bound in Canada

McClelland & Stewart Ltd.
The Canadian Publishers
481 University Avenue
Toronto, Ontario
M5G 2E9
www.mcclelland.com

1 2 3 4 5   07 06 05 04 03

Frances Isabel Horton McKillop

1900–1989

Contents

LOOP

LITTLE STORIES

I

The cherries are just turning
from green to ripe
translucent red, almost hidden
by the leaves.
You're speaking of love and how it spends
itself or changes,
                         depending

on what's at stake. Take that ancient tale,
you say, knight and lady,
husband

II

and wife. I know the way it goes.
He leaves.
And there's someone else,
there always is.
                    The cherries, miniature

III

purses,
are nearly covered by the leaves.

But he's willing
to let her go,
so gives everything, gives her up.

                              It's reached that point
when twilight softens,
gets into corners,
waits in the hush of branch and leaf, waits.

IV

Now the fork on the plate is shadowed
mauve.
          She's tricked
by the one
who says he loves her.

V

                              No, it's more than that.
There's a trick inside the trick,
hand drawing hand
erasing hand: her husband finding out
how much he cares. Love discovering
what it is at the expense
of what it was.

2

VI

Looking into itself, again and again.

VII

There's a kind of love that needs
to keep
its distance. Take anything,
take dog and moon.
                    Take the howl that empties
the heart. Take the heart,
your own heart.

VIII

No. Let's not look
at the moon, effortlessly
rising behind the birch.
                    Lavishing itself
on anyone who notices. Always
coming into it.

IX

Moon: quartered, halved, less than,
more. The part that you can't see.

Drink
what's left.

X

Things don't stay the same. I can't see
the tree now. Cherry, plum.
I can't
see the roses, their leaves slightly
yellow, because of mites,
or the daisies, black-eyed Susans,
shrivelled heads of peonies.

XI

It's gone a deeper blue. I see only
edges, one blurred with another. We can make the tale
whatever we want: I see you,
but you're different.
                              There's your hand
on the table

XII

                              almost hidden.
What was it we said
about endings? Even your voice
has the dark in it, full

4

of gardens
at night, lawns without fences,
something brushing through the grass,
flicking its tail. The door

                            opening

and shutting.
                All these things

XIII

we can't say.

A NAME, MANY NAMES

I knew you
long before I saw you,
one thing inside another
making itself up. Lightly,
snow fell, kept falling
the night you were born —
like those prayers tied
to branches by the Japanese —
scissored bits of paper,
each one a word:
a name, many names, loose
in the dark.

Later you'll need a name
that's door and window, roof
and bed. You'll need a name to foil
the thief that comes
to live in your heart. But now
you need a name so diaphanous
and small
it takes its shape from air.

NOW WHAT?

When the gates open everyone rushes
past the garden where someone – fenced in –
kneels to check the sprinklers. We keep
close as bees
alongside the paddlewheel boat
and Tom Sawyer's Island
all the way to Splash Mountain,
temporarily closed. A woman circles
with a baby in a pink stroller. Now what?
Even Cinderella's Castle
is under repair. Things glazed with heat
waver, diminishing in size. Snow White,
with her paste-coloured skin, cherry lips,
is perspiring. Here's the Mouse
with a helper, who says anyone wanting autographs
has to line up. I watch, under the jacarandas
in the heavy, perfumed air,
rubbing a little dirt between my fingers
to see if it's real.

At night we ride the bus back – swaying
from side to side – to our hotel, wearily
picking our way through towels by the pool
shaped like a guitar, where children are jumping,
wreathed in sparkles of water. Up they go
and down, every little jewel.
In the shadows of the rose garden,
a skinny girl in a white bathing suit

tells her boyfriend – her voice high,
harsh – that she came here to have fun.

On the last morning, we see a huge tree –
made entirely by hand – at the centre
of another theme park, the newest and best.
Stilt-walkers plumed in yellow and blue
stalk around us like spoonbills.
It's the hottest day yet.
No shade. A child flings
a video camera on the ground. Stupid bugger,
shrieks a woman, then a man scoops up the boy,
gives him a bottle of juice, whether
he wants it or not. The peacock imitates
his cry. I hold my children's hands
so tightly they ask to be released. They'd like
water, but I have none. Over there
lions are splayed
on artificially warmed rocks, and giraffes
stagger through landscaped forests,
heads moving this way and that
with the slightly lunatic and bewildered look
of things captured
on *America's Funniest Home Videos*. And it's late, it's late –
perhaps we'll miss the quaint little train
that takes us to the African village
where we run all the way to the exit,
smiling and nodding
at the bus driver who asks
how we liked it
as we sink down on the plastic seats.

THE WATER CLOCK

What a wonder! The clock inside a tower,
driven by a water wheel, dividing the fluid
day into hours. Anyone climbing to the top,
gazing at the hills around Khaifeng
might have said to her children,
Look, here's the future. A gilded thing,

with little bells and drums marking
minutes, pronouncing
progress. Su Sung's marvellous clock
set up for the world
to see, with celestial globe
and armillary sphere — one revolution
each day, the passage of

water measured by weight
and counterweight, as darkness balances
light. What can't be seen
always comes: Tartars took the clock in its tower
one century later, transported it
to Peking, where lightning
struck the armillary sphere, where it finally

stopped working altogether,
and another century or so afterwards
the Mongol emperor — no, it wasn't melted down
just then — wandered around it,
imagining what it was: water's voice
slipped through a wheel so time could talk.

This is not tenderness: lilacs hanging in the rain,
      my breath
coming in gasps, the dog shaking herself beside me.
      I'm thinking of the slap

in the day when the light goes. The puncture, a sigh
      of something pricked
by a blue that has no edge. Your lungs, collapsed
      bubbles, whatever

draws air, keeps us going. She found the keys, drove you
      to Emergency
in her stocking feet. Into that rising panic —
      a snap: any flower

broken from its branch. Along with this: the mauve,
      dark purple, wealth
of the new. Rain, fathering the blooms. Here,
      everything

I've been so slow to offer up. All those hours
      spent reading
the mirror. A little cloud, exhaled, distorts every
      reflection. We're not kings,

or fools, or third daughters. We're only the makings
      of ourselves. You,

with a cord trailing on the carpet, one end for oxygen,
      one for the body,

like the snake's tail, the swallowed circle, that keeps
      this hour, this rain,
each opened bud alive. Yanking the leash,
      the dog pulls me on

to something else, her nose deep in beaded grass.
      Then down the hill
on Brookland and round the bend, my hand burning
      wet from the lilacs.

THE BLUE HOUR

after "The God Forsakes Antony" by Constantine Cavafy

In that blue hour, something calls you
from sleep, summons you to the window.
The ink-glossed lake:
night. A shimmer, dancers
twining, one into
another. It's late. This dread,
how did it find its way in? Lock the door,
draw the curtains almost

closed. Music, far-off. You
could be in a hotel, anywhere,
with people sipping drinks below, on a balcony.
A chinking of ice, conversation
mingled with laughter. Warmth,
faint perfume. Traces
of a dream. Now the wind rises, takes
shape. How white it is – a warning –
snow, exquisitely
strafing the dark. Rumours

of war. In the morning
it's cold, but each breath translates
as a plume, a prancing horse.
Whatever comes,
let it come. The gods scatter
reminders wherever they go. High up,

a peak. A helmet. Breastplates
of gold. Light, new-fallen on the path.
Goodbye. The branches of the Douglas fir,
those sentinels, guard
some bright city of the air.

NORTH

Into the wind, then,
as the trees bend, blackly,
against evening's indigo. This is where mind goes
when it wishes itself wider.

Unmapped
place of silences.
                    Where the wind sharpens itself.

                    North lacks balance,
and whatever hangs in it, about to be
decided. Lacks furniture, trinkets, opera
on the radio, a certain
je ne sais quoi. Most humourless
of directions,
yet most honest, pulling the compass needle
back to itself, back
home.

SOUTH

Into the arms of
vistas, seas
retiring from the beach, deliberately
as hands sliding from a table. The solace
that it's winter
up north. Direction of delights, of lies,
away and down the map
into fantasy: swirling dresses and men with pistols
on the wide porches. You go ahead,
my darling. No matter what happens

                                          we'll improvise.
Driving all night, past newlywed nooks,
roller-coaster parks,
rest havens – strung with coloured Christmas lights –
for the abandoned, where rust begins
a new life for itself. It's not the end
of desire, just the beckoning
cruise ship of somewhere,
somewhere else.

Goddess of beginnings: naïve
light in an eggshell sky.
All new: not yet,
not quite. Hiding what it knows,
offering its slender
arms, spiritual neck. Offering
pretty rooms of childhood —
with the scent of cut grass
through open windows — each

                    breath,
                    tooth,
                    star.

East thins into
what's around the corner: west.
It gives itself up, every last secret,
Sumerian tablets, fragments
of Ming porcelain, dust on the Silk Road.

                    But this is where it happened,
the cradle of it all: garden
of belief.

Westing into sunset, the spectacular
finale of day. Git along,
little dogie.
Tinted rose-red, the great moraines,
cirques – those pleasure bowls – and mountains
softening into twilight,
that place we can't reach. Over here,
the king's tents, his encamped
armies. Civilization –
with its wheels and spears,
windmills, catapults, and clocks –
all rolling this way. Tag along
with trucks, trailers, the coast-to-coast
road show. All going west,
                     direction of endings

or second chances. No turning back, dear,
the iron's unplugged, door's locked.
Take some photographs by the giant walleye,
or next to the car before it gives up the ghost. In this light,
we can part the velvet
curtain, disappear.

THE NEW YEAR

Someone dragged our Christmas tree
onto the bonfire. A blaze of white-gold, sudden
heat. The slender branches curled like fingers,
clutching and clutching
what was already gone. We stood close
together on the snowy edge of beach.
My son was scrolling Happy
New Year in the air with sparklers,
and my daughter writing her name,
as if it might stay there.

On the point, someone lit fireworks
– red, green, yellow – like handkerchiefs
plucked out of a top hat. They went up,
down. *Phfft.* Overhead, the stars
stayed in their places. The night was cold,
so cold, and for a moment I saw time –
century on century – frozen into place. Nothing
moved. They could have been under the glassy ice,

those things from the past. A howl
stopped in the throat. A thin child running, naked,
down a road. No going back for anything.
But then someone reached over
and kissed me. I offered
a bouquet of sparklers
to my son, who threw it,
joyously, across the icy harbour.
A tiny, extravagant flourish.

The Triumph of Death

These watches. Ticking, still. Each hour is cold:
the rims surround quick voices. Shut in rooms.
Gone. *Tick*. The towers. *Tock*. Of fire. A fold
in air. We're smoke, drifting. A painted doom
where cities burn and ships go down. Death's
dark sky — a grainy docudrama. Time
swings bones on circus wheels. Listen: wind's breath,
a shriek. *Theatrum Mundi*. In their prime,
the living. Leapt. That buckling of the knees.
Then gunshots: plastic bags on fences. Snapping.
Or loose. *Thank you — shop — at*. The lovers see
nothing. He plays a lute. She sings. Clapping —
machines sift through debris for the remains.
A sales receipt, a shoe. The silvery rain.

Landscape with the Parable of the Sower

A sales receipt, a shoe. The silvery rain
has many hands. A stream – Fresh Kills – elides
with river. Thick and slow. A landfill plain:
a ghost in biohazard gear. Gulls ride
the thermals, circling high as barges come,
a linking chain. Blue metropolis, far-
off glints of light. The cranes all lift and hum,
making hills of metal, bone. Crushed cars.
So garbage rises: this stench is monument.
Yet Brueghel's farmer takes the seeds, flings wide
his arm. A miracle: small event. We meant
to go, but every boat was laden. Tides
pulled home, pulled here, then left us for the birds.
We take the shape of soil, abandon words.

The Tower of Babel I

We take the shape of soil, abandon words.
The world will change without us. Did we glean
a little shine? Perhaps. These wheeling birds
drift down to earth. Crying. The air, unseen,
seeks entry without keys. All locked, shut down.
A spackled light gets through. We merely craved
a taste. *Hello, my name is* _____. A crown,
a king. One makes the other into slave.
Behind is Babel's core. Red as a heart
opened for bypass. Laid bare. Wind, idling.
It's quiet. Still. The horses, loaded carts,
are stuck. The ships, the docks. Thin bridles
of cloud. All stopped. Each thing unclocked, undone.
A man who kneels to plead his case. Warm sun.

The Tower of Babel II

That man who knelt to plead his case, that sun:
they're gone. In time, air hardens, growing dark.
The wars go on; beyond the TV, guns
talk to themselves. One, two. They whisper, bark.
Erotica. And Babel: height's desire
is weary of itself, but there's no end
to greed. A cruise, a condo. Guests for hire.
On the rug: a shirt, a shoe. Whatever bends
one body to another. We've forgotten.
Those painted clouds are knives. Slipped in walls
between the ribs. This plot device: rotten —
the thing exploded from within. Small
papers, white flakes. Last wish. Someone's cellphone.
("Are you still there? *Are you?*") A voice falls. Stone.

The Slaughter of the Innocents

"Are you still there? *Are you?*" A voice falls. Stone,
unbearable stone. It grinds. It tastes of grief.
Don't watch. Go blind. Oh Lord, those moans
will haunt us. This one. That one there. Brief
lives. Snow. And here, between the black trees, blood.
A leaping dog. A bird. Everywhere we turn
there's whiteness in the air. And memory, a flood
of killings no kindness can assuage. Urns
half-full of ashes: nothing that we knew
of those we loved. So young. Such shining hair,
those gleams recalled. A silence follows through
the rooms of when and how. Now, up the stairs
a rescuer is climbing. But he's too late.
And look what happened. This. Short straw of fate.

Who knows what happened? A short straw of fate,
all that. Years ago. But now we've changed;
those terrors tucked back in the heart. "Just great,
that weekend special: everything arranged."
We return; the house looks strange. Each thing
deceives. The counters, cutlery. Believe
the chairs; they guard the table in a ring.
The hunters come. They're trudging, slow. Reprieve
makes curving flight, a song in evening's sky:
pale green at dusk. Some children skate; they laugh.
And history has no place. Easy to lie
on queen-sized beds, *dream a little dream*. Half-
heard, the phantoms speak: No, you weren't there —
We turn; we sleep. But once there was a prayer.

Christian and the Adulteress

We turn; we sleep. But once there was a prayer,
a way to finger mystery. It floats,
one plastic bag, freed from the fence, that snare
with loops of wire. We translate into motes,
a glimmer in a shaft of sun. One glide,
we're gone. A painted scene: against this plea
is set a stone. An end. Each thing is tried.
A man makes notes in sand. The wind goes free.
One gust: his words are ghosts. The dust, absolved,
has vanished too. First kiss, last glance. *Tick. Tock.*
All goes to ground. We kneel down and dissolve.
Turn in. Turn out of time. Where nothing's clocked.
A touch: so light. Love's breath. Things we can't hold:
these watches. Ticking. Still. Each hour is cold.

A MANY SPLENDOURED THING

It takes up the full screen, getting more and more attention. Drive-in, drive-through, drive away. Swallow it all, the taste. Not remembered with a *sweet, sweet, sweet.* Nothing like that. There's a turquoise bay near Hong Kong where they filmed the movie. A candy-pink hotel. Love sliding away like a disease from the arms of this one, that one, lips pressed against water. There are beggars there, living on junks with brown sails, even now.

Give the guy a picnic, a chance to fondle old memories with his sister. Let him have tranquil green crisscrossed by hedgerow and a ruin in the distance. Give him what he needs: a chance to open up. Talk about clear skies of recollection. Oh how. And how. Most beautiful heart leaping up, little heart fish. Make those common sights of earth so like a cloud.

How it wants to say to itself: Victory! Think of it as an ironclad ship, the CSS *Virginia*, covered in pig fat so the shells will slide away. This is the way you defend what's true. Even if your legs are shot off, you must pull the lanyard on the cannon. Pull it, for God's sake. Meanwhile the *Cumberland* — a fighting sloop — is going down, decks wet with blood and pieces of leg and arm. The drummer boy lives, because of his drum, which he uses as a raft.

Pharaoh Djoser's still in there, getting dustier. You can visit him in his pyramid on the Saqqara Plateau. How he aches! There's a hole for him to see by, cut in the rock. He can see each star. He can see the breath of the gods, so tender and faintly white against the flood of night. All this time he's been imagining things, a way to get out. Haven't you been told love is patient?

It turns, inevitably, to madness. You wake and see the socks lying on the bureau. The photograph of your daughter vanished from the frame. You thought you listened to her. Now you wind yourself in the cloth of suffering, cloth of twilight, but it does no good. All you wanted was a gift. Something fine and silvery, that did not pierce you.

Can't you feel that touch of wind against your brow, lifting your hair? And the cities of light beneath you? This is what you wanted, riding on the wing of darkness. Go anywhere you want: back to childhood, forward to your children's children's children. Every star a door. Every door open.

After the paramilitaries carried out their work in Ljubenic, they returned. Who was left? A two-year-old, a pregnant girl, a six-year-old, a ninety-year-old woman, a few of the crippled and mentally disabled. The sky remains immense, impervious. You won't find them in the folds of the mountains, in the lichen that clings to the rocks, in the curled ferns. The trees say nothing. They hold up their arms.

If men had not walked on the moon. No small step, giant leap for the ghosts wavering on the television's snowy screen. No slow, graceful bounds through space. No one conquering the unknown, planting flags here and there in the dark.

The lion is wearing away. The stars are loose. But the heads of the statues remain, each telling glory. There was a king who ruled the earth, and now he lives beneath it, in a cave of treasures. You'll never find it, say the broken heads, whitened by rain, by sun. No one has come close. Go into the tunnels of your own heart — any cave you are afraid to enter — and strike a match.

Let's be wide as this and round. We'll build ourselves *senza armadura*, in concentric circles: higher, higher. A circle within an octagon: one dome outside, another within. A staircase winding between, so tourists marvel as they climb to the top, startling the pigeons. Air beaten to thin gold by many wings.

Draw not just one part of it, but the whole. Yes, even the three-dimensional way someone turns, blinking away tears. Do not think too much of surfaces (instructs Nicolaides). There's something else, but the eye alone is not capable. In any case, get it down on paper. Let's say it's sorrow. Let's say it's a little bit of death getting into it. Well, get that on paper too.

THE GRAND CANYON

I haven't gone there: tell me what you've seen.
The air stretched taut, the cross-stitch work of birds.
We think we know it, but we've never been

any place where we could practise how to lean,
wide open, hungry for the stars, sky's tongue.
I haven't gone there: tell me what you've seen.

Of course it's not quite real, like childish dreams:
the bright-blue dragonflies, the lips they sew.
We think we know it, but we've never been.

We live too far. It might be shut, unseen,
that mouth – voiceless – its stories undisclosed.
I haven't gone there: tell me what you've seen

standing at the edge, taking in the scene
as silence falls, a blue past blue. It's then
we think we know it, but we've never been.

When moonlight seeps inside it's so serene,
so deep. Half-full of liquid we can't drink.
I haven't gone there: tell me what you've seen.
We think we know it, but we've never been.

The bald eagle looks down from the elm —
the skin of the dead tree gone shiny, smooth —
fixing its gaze, eight times more
acute, on my head. We take what
omens we find: months ago — a moonless night,

cold and still — foxes in a ring
around a cat. Who wants to see
the closing of that circle? Last night I dreamed
of fingers gently combing my hair. Asking,
calling. Ghosts of hands.
A far-off cry. The long, uncanny

screech of an animal pulled to pieces. Nothing
kind about portents. They take us to the edge
of a witching place where the snowy lawns
are lipped with shadows. Or
they haul us into the middle, everything
ranged around us quietly, so quietly.

ALMOST SOLSTICE

There's a picket of spruce at the top
of the hill, the moon a lock in evening's

gate. Each of us lit by the simplest
moments. Glimmering in the grass one by

one: fireflies. Don't say a word and look
for what can't be seen among aspens and grass,

rich with shadow. Our hands smell of sage,
of wolf willow, all those things asked

and never asked. Cedars fill the air with a casual
scent of warmth and home, where dark is shaping

itself as a shoulder, an arm. There's still a dusky gold
light in the west, spruce lifting skirts in a little gust

of wind, settling, nesting, cry of owlets, snort
of deer, fields dense with buzz and chortle,

whirligig noises of carnival. Sleep,
sleep — between shooting-star flowers and clover,

this blade of grass or that, the creek winding
through like a thought that's almost forgotten

in the sedges and bog violets — until morning,
when nothing will find us but sky.

after Grant McConnell's *A Cautionary Fable: We Are Not Dancing*, 1991 (acrylic on wood)

What's left:
claws, dark fur, cable of spine.
The twisted bits lie on the path
                          and the dog plays with it,
shaking her glossy head.

I've seen the remains of this body,
day after day,
on the path at the Landing. Each time the dog
pounces on it and I warn her off,
                              shout
to make her stop. It's only fur and claws:
nothing at all,

but we've felt teeth at our own necks,
been dragged, bitten,
ripped open.
                    Staggering
to our feet —
feral, bloody — we know how it ends.
And it ends.

Still, there's a glitter
of light along the sedges,

                the heron making a slapstick
appearance, turtle dunking into water,

where it can't be seen, can't be heard,
can't be thought.

I slice into the pomegranate:
my son is the first to take a piece. He eats
it whole. Now my daughter
picks out seeds, bites them one by one. The juice
runs over her hands, drips onto the table. Bright
red, it could be something pulled
from the body, still pulsing.
I pick it up, hold it, sweetness
sliding down my wrists.
                              Think of entering
the pomegranate,
strange realm at the end
of things, where icebergs might be
turned in the lathe of impossibly
deep water. A place that lures
with frozen shelves, lustrous
cliffs, and beyond, always beyond,
a snowy cave where the seeds hang –
ruby stalactites – just out of reach.

Both children put out stained hands
and I cut more for them, discard the rind.
This is the fruit of Hades, I tell them.
Persephone ate a pomegranate – she couldn't
resist – and stayed in that kingdom,

a darkened room
at twilight.
                              She could be anyone at all
sitting in an armchair after a bath,
by the uncurtained window, seeing
the stars as locks, each frosted blade of grass
a key. Too much distance
between things.

How densely packed this fruit:
pirated jewels strewn on the breadboard.
Here's the last of it. When we get up
we've changed a little.

                    Somewhere,
a woman sits in darkness
– deep in her own myth –
clasps the collar of an old robe,
never thinking to turn on a lamp.
She waits. You wouldn't think she remembers
hope, but there are days
when she floats right out the window, suspended
in light. You have to look at her,
covering your eyes at the same time,
as you would during an eclipse.

Night was woven through with what we said,
a Persian rug, patterned with random stars.
We sat on the windowsill of a ruined
farmhouse, all of us quiet after talking.
Weeds lay tangled below, a great square
of something intricate, unknown,
and I thought how it could be caught
by four corners: a carpet lifted
into the dark, undulating up and up.
I might have been pulled into the blue-black,
too high, too far, but something called me

back. Yesterday, kayaking, I recalled it
near a silver stretch where herons gather
at low tide. Just beyond,
water runs deeper, faster, the eel grass
slowly brushed this way and that, farther
down. We'd paddled back the wrong way,
though I liked the shallows and then
the cool green deeps. There, before us, birds
ascended as if drawing something
with them, the sheen of water, a wavering
transparency. We could see the slant
of fields, scattered houses and barns,
orange buoys comically bobbing,
and currents opening to reveal,
lower down, many liquid stairways.

                              We nearly missed it,
the heron lifting slowly –
with Churchillian effect –
                         into the air.

The cordgrass stings bare feet,
                              wind loosens the heart
with only a gust. It stands open
to the endlessness of ocean, to wild
roses by the road leading away
into a pale unwinding.

                         All this time
the dog's been racing up and down
the beach, covered in sand. A few people
stand in silky water to their waists,
not moving. Something breaks us
in half when we least
expect it.
                    Latch the heart
when you go out,
or it'll keep on banging.

In night's cloak
the creatures are quiet and furred,
buzzing or slow.

        The owl, glove-soft
over the creek,
hunting for food.
A scurrying, a blow,
something clutched at the neck.

Folded over and under
night
     is demand.

Devour, devour. Night is screech and cry:
more
and still more. Taste,

kill.
A sliver of bone on the path.

        Owl eats mouse,
night eats day: god on a plate
again
    and again.

Whose?

This is a boy's body. Visited, like Sainte-Thérèse, by visions.

On his wrist

are many heads of obscure Chinese scholars, buried to their necks in sand. You might think of the heads as attached to bodies, or sliced from them by a dozen swordsmen.

There are tiny dots to represent the hundred heads. Or perhaps the dots signify the sand, in which the heads have disappeared.

On his left thigh

Alexander's famous phalanx, a box formation (moving hedge of bodies) that saved the Greeks.

Who was it they were fighting?

On his right toe

is a tiny face, but not one any of us know. (It could be a miniature portrait of the nameless woman who lived on the Steppes and rode a horse as well as any man, hunted with falcons, and had six children before she was twenty-four. When her youngest child died, she put two pieces of felt over its eyes, as she had done with five others.)

On his neck

a miniature human body, bird-headed creature from the caves of Lascaux.

Was there ever such a thing?

On his right earlobe

Jumbo the elephant, killed on the railway tracks in St. Thomas, Ontario, in 1885, squeezed between two trains. Its tusks became scimitars piercing its brain, but it did not die right away.

Something remains.

On his left eyelid

a symbol for Planck time that can't be deciphered easily. More beautiful than the Big Bang itself,

this tattoo, and more original.

The body

is that of a boy killed in a convenience store in a small town.

The murderer was a few years older, wearing a death's head mask, carrying a hunting knife.

A tattoo of wounds.

How perfect the flesh, just

before a body is cremated.

History is whatever
lingers.

Feel the body slip under its own locked gate:

> can't,
>
> don't,
>
> won't.

Nothing slow,
nothing too quick: shiver of light
over water, night's choreography.
Each leading step,
sure and measured:

> tap, trip, one-step, two-step, foxtrot, waltz,

then
long, long, together, getting the hang of it – short,
short – and long, long, together round the floor
until it ends. The lake is framed in the windows,
struck gold, poised.

Ladies, rouge to rouge, tenderly
holding each other up: a pair of cards,
and the guy with the red satin shirt, fancy
shoes. Begin again,
one step partnered with another, the discreet festival
of heel, toe, skim, slide
apart. Return,

arm to waist, palm to palm, recalling
rhyme. Not only this, but
body made into bell,

shimmering
with its thousand echoes
                              and whatever sleeps inside echoes,

even after it's over, and the screen door slams
warm, slams cool.
Everyone vanishes – someone kicks a can,
someone else laughs –
into the dark, needled with fireflies.

FINALLY

The cottonwood – sprayed
within an inch of its life –
still offers up
its small gift of beads,

                 green and mysterious.

Everything a rosary, even the broken
strands of cloud. Anyone could be flayed
by light here, stretched
on a rack of field. Someone rides a bicycle
on the dirt road. The bees
are restless inquisitors in their hives. It's clear
finally –
         why there is too much

rain, or not enough.

                 But look, since we have no words

for this – no devotions –

I'll prepare
the moth's body in a linen
handkerchief, diminutive
shroud.

And the bells continue on the hour. Time
falls to pieces,
               one,
                    two,
                          three.

How it starts, how it ends: a wild tuft in the sky, a cloud. This blue.

Floating. We take whatever shape we find. We learn each fold in air.

What we know best is what we want. Open palm of moon. Gone.

Breath. The next and then. We've run out of a little clock of words.

Only this: one hand over another, our hearts folded like wings, sleep.

———

Small, smaller on a white bed. Each breath a country, a border. Love.

Waking. We could be envelopes or knives. Instead we're simple as cups:

_____

everything and nothing. Time is what we leave: your hands, your body . . .

we're filled, yet we tip constantly. Goodbye. As for happiness —

---

it spills itself. The petal of a violet, a blue ear, listening. How easily

it spills itself. The petal of a violet, a blue ear, listening. How easily

_____

we're filled, yet we tip constantly. Goodbye. As for happiness —

everything and nothing. Time is what we leave: your hands, your body . . .

Waking. We could be envelopes or knives. Instead we're simple as cups:

Small, smaller on a white bed. Each breath a country, a border. Love.

Only this: one hand over another, our hearts folded like wings, sleep.

Breath. The next and then. We've run out of a little clock of words.

———————————————————————————————————————

What we know best is what we want. Open palm of moon. Gone.

Floating. We take whatever shape we find. We learn each fold in air.

How it starts, how it ends: a wild tuft in the sky, a cloud. This blue.

He yanks your body, falling hard, an axe
– one ringing blow – and he's on top of you,
a hand pushed hard against your face. Then whacks
his cock between your legs. He'll kill you too:
that cord will strangle, cut. He'll do it. Soon.
Those snaps – no, don't! – of kids taped to his dash.
Oh God! That car. The fear, the crazy moon,
a clutch on wrist, and night shut like a sash.
He's done. Now. Rolling over, gets the cord.
No, wait. His kids are how old – what'd he say?
They're five and eight. He knots, unknots the cord,
tells more: his wife and kids, the fucked-up way
things go. And then he's gone: you hear the car.
Listen. Your heart. A spoon inside a jar.

So large: a wide mouth, open, containing
all of us. We were watching baseball,
a distant game played between tiny people
far below. The grass, a carpet of soft plastic turf,
was eerily green and the players, positioned
here and there, knew what to do. The crowd,
satisfied with chips and beer, rose up clapping
from time to time, calculating when to stand
and when to sit, so that a row rippled
as if a wind had blown through, except

wind did not come into this place. Only
a strip of August sky was visible, cathedrals
of cloud piled above us. On the Jumbotron
people were looking for themselves, waving
in the wrong direction, facing away
from the camera. It tracked them with the diligent
scrutiny of Dante, in section after section,
one great circle upon another. Things fell
into place decisively: the outfielder caught the fly
ball, perfecting the arc by snapping his glove shut.

And how carelessly the boy carrying a cooler
of drinks made change beside us, jingling coins
into our palms. He paused for an instant
to catch the double play. Now the home team
was up to bat, top of the sixth. It started to rain,
so the last of the sky vanished, slowly,

as the roof of the dome moved overhead, locking
precisely. Tell me a story, I wanted to shout
to the players, about the magic in that ball,

thrown so swiftly to the pitcher. Nothing
could be said. It's true there was a story: rising
action, shot by smoothly rolling television cameras,
media people clustered on the sidelines. A climax — yes,
and resolution, possibly the kind that moved
the heart. One or two pitchers who hadn't made it
into the game stood in the bullpens, making do
with invisible balls, things that could barely
be discerned. They might have been tossing doves
without dropping them. They had the spirit

of being in it together, ignoring the fact
they'd soon be devoured by something
crouching in the shadows. Perhaps they waited
for the gods, who weren't attending. It didn't matter
that we were still watching. It was over;
our team had lost. Lights furred each head,
swathed the field so its acute symmetry
lay before us, as in a vision. It disappeared
when we went out into the night, where the rain,
leaving small handprints on everything, had ended.

A MOOR, RAIN

Somewhere, down a dirt road,
a man flings open a screen door,
goes outside. He's shouting.

A woman is inside, crying. Small
sounds, like mice
behind baseboards. A few
moments ago she was shouting too.
Maybe she threw something.
A radio. A plate.

❧

He stops shouting,
lets rain touch him, run
under his collar.
Lets himself be rain.

She sits on the floor.
Her feet are bare. The house
is full of shouting, now
that it's stopped.

❧

He goes outside
and the house turns into a hut.

It's the same as it always was.

❦

She looks at her bare feet.
At bits of plate on the floor.
It's not enough.
If she'd taken all the plates
and thrown them at the wet, black sky
— the wall of night —
it wouldn't have been enough.

❦

In a bedroom a child, the youngest,
perhaps the oldest, watches
rain come down the window
in glistening, unreal paths.

❦

The man goes out
and when he comes back inside
it's all changed.

❦

Or maybe nothing
happened. A man, a woman,
sitting in chairs, reading. Separate islands

of light cast by the lamps. Silence,
round as a plate.

ↀ

He comes back into the house
bringing the moor with him.

ↀ

The children are as far away from him
as they can get.

The furniture stands
where it always stood. Waiting.

The refrigerator opens and shuts
as usual, closing itself on something.

ↀ

His wife has gone to bed.

He's never going back to that bed.

She's awake, listening to him
never coming back to bed.

LOT'S WIFE

This is the woman you don't know,
— unnamed, undone —
though you've heard how she turned
for a last look and that
was that. No time
for those twelve chapters
to creative awakening, with accompanying
exercises. Lot kept his head
down. Why is it that a woman can't
give up what's already gone? We all know
what curiosity plus cat equals. This time

God snapped his fingers,
reduced the cities to ash,
along with two of Lot's daughters, sons-in-law,
twins in the polka-dot stroller,
rattles on the rug,
a whatnot full of souvenirs:
the straw donkey from Spain, clay vase
from Mexico with the crack in it. Dishes
still in the sink, phone off the hook
and the voice of the angel
echoing loud in everyone's ears.
Told you so.

                                    After that

who was left
to pick up the pieces? Soon Lot was sleeping

with his younger daughters,
but it was all so dreamlike. Across the plain,
the city kept burning. People made little cries
of distress, flames leapt
from one building
to another. Smoke filled the air.

They're searching for what remains of a man and two women.
     You've heard the news:
they found suitcases, pills in bottles, little things that don't matter.
     What everyone wants is their beauty,

now they've taken it. After forty-eight hours it's still unconfirmed, but
     women are already weeping
across the country for the child recalled on television, saluting the flag-
     draped coffin

and taking his mother's black-gloved hand. They knew one day
     he'd resemble
his father, in this hour of the nation, home of the brave. Myths
     have a way of lulling us

with inflatable ease. Anything will do: a beckoning ocean on a sunny day
     in July, idle and devoid
of clues about what might have happened, might have in each thoughtless
     wave. Things wash up

on the sand, described every hour on the hour, so he'll die many times,
     replayed with Greek effect.
(In the motorcade in Dallas, the men were thrust forward, back, almost
     comically,

while a woman in a perfect suit — spattered with blood, bits of flesh — reached
     out her hand for help

as she climbed over the seats.) It's the end of another day; something fades
    into grey, keeps fading, and diminishes.

ᘒᘓ

I spent one summer night — too hot to turn over, too hot to sleep — dreaming
    of a plane dipping
over a glassy sea, the sky hazy and suffused with the glow of evening.
    All night

I flew into a lip between air and ocean, an ending without the usual shocks,
    only embrace,
those arms of indolence. This morning they announced the deaths,
    referring to temperature and time —

twelve hours, eighteen — that anyone could survive. But we all knew
    it happened instantly, and then
one body trailed another down, water passing over them, through them
    like combs. One woman's hair, loose

and pretty, fanned around her face as she descended, leaving parties
    under the stars, guests mingling
on a level, grassy lawn, while a pleasure boat drifted in the bay — sails slack —
    leaving a foamless wake.

ᘒᘓ

Go back. The final moment comes when the plane, high up, swivels
    upside down, without horizon,
that plausible, straight line, and hangs, hangs — about to descend, spiralling
    crazily — while the mind

73

clings to its shelf of rattling trinkets. What can't be happening is.
       And is
and is. Until it can't be thought. The doves of rescue fail;
       we take our leave. But remember

that private world of detail. Think of her coming downstairs in the small
       hours, imagine her
in a nightgown, face pale in the light of the fridge. The way he used to sleep
       with his arms flung wide

across the rumpled sheets, duvet on the floor: ordinary lives are always
       embellished by the papers.
Distance magnifies or shrinks — a plane, a toy lost from a pocket — either way,
       something's gone for good.

THE IMPERIAL ASYLUM

after a photograph by Charles Nègre, *Refectory at the Imperial Asylum, Vincennes*, 1858-59
(salted paper print from glass negative)

ை

Light comes through the long windows,
making the people stranded here
seem like they've forgotten
something, perhaps misplaced a bill.
How quietly they stand: the convalescent
with the goatee and cap, and – duplicated
like an image in a mirror – another man
behind him, both of them staring
as if they've seen us, as if they understand

illusions, any of time's card tricks.
We're disguised at the tables where we sit
eating, or sipping a drink. Think how close
we are, all of us, crowded together,
or wandering in circles. And how we're
caught in the blur of movement
as someone shakes his head. Or how we stand,
resolute, but entirely without purpose,
in this light, this streaming, gentle light.

ை

There are moments when we find ourselves
— after that step off the cliff —
in mid-air, like a cartoon character
that scoots back to solid ground
in exaggerated fright, or drops
right through the earth, leaving a hole
outlining the shape of shock. This is where
it happened. Everything

goes down with us when we fall,
the teacher with the glass eye in grade four,
a dead puppy on the road, a few unwanted
wedding gifts — cups and coffee pots —
a baby newly born, wailing
in our arms. All this and more,
in the place where we find ourselves:
a room full of shadows moving as we do,
haltingly, every bone broken.

೧೦

What are you afraid of? This:
they take me on a tour
starting at Ward Five, top floor of Penrose.
Bars on the window. Women rocking
wildly in chairs, pulling at their hair.
A few of them circle, naked, around
and around a few squares of yellow tile.

There's a large man to guard them,
reading comics at a table.

Through tiny openings between the bars:
bits of lawn, fragments
of lake. The tip of Wolfe Island.

One winter a girl vanishes,
leaves the workshop, trudges through
snow to the shattered
edge of lake. Ice tossed into teeth,
spires, handles. Beyond, the wide
floor, hard as linoleum. It's March,
when the ice — unpredictably — heaves
and cracks and keens
a weird, high song. It dances her,
lifts and holds her. Nothing to fear

ॐ

except fear itself. What can't be
seen, can't be
known. A scientist, working at Chernobyl
after the fact. Gradually, his face
acquires the look of the dead,
a mask: hollow cheeks, tight lips,
eyes that see through

the living. One night he sits down
outside the lab and doesn't get up.
His relatives collect his body
from a village morgue.
Legs. Arms. Smell of death
and ammonia. Here is the body

of a man whose head was stitched, badly.
Stomach and chest opened. Each organ
taken, but not a plastic bag
to put them in. And no one
on these tables any of us would recognize.

≈

Fear of what's next: unseen,
a woman cries
in a car, bent over, unable
to stop. This is somewhere near
St. Thomas, named for the patron saint
of the side of the road,
where corn is tasselled, leafed,
hidden greenly in husks.

She's not in a car parked by a field;
she's on a ledge. Below, there is only
all the way down, and above, in a sleeve
of sky, the many-feathered angels
who will not descend.

≈

It's quiet here.
The elms will take you in their arms,
and if you want to weep,
weep. But grief has to have its end
somewhere, in this curve
where the river slides

78

around a stony island. The heron moves one gilded leg
after another, steps like a courtier across
a blue throne room.

You can go as far as you like,
to the edge of the harbour, asylum of cordgrass.
Silence. Wind moves small hands on the water,
fingers the tidal pool. Can you see
the others in the distance — the one there
and the one standing behind him?
They're all here; they stand with us
in the light that falls like this,
like that,
through alders and cattails, onto the path.

THE TRAILER PARK

I

In the middle of town, a trailer park,
RVs in comfortable rows like cows
waiting to be milked. Coloured lanterns
hang from awnings, and in the soft evening
a man wrestles with his son, laughing:
Come on, be a man. Voices see-saw.
That you, honey?
On the little bridge joining one side
of the park to the other – green living rooms –
a teenager, bicycling, loses his balance
and topples sideways. The child strapped
into the seat on the back screams
as she falls. Her helmet bangs against
the railing in slow motion. She's

all right. But just for a moment
she sees the world divided
into ceiling and doors. Floor.
Sky. Wallpaper
of stars.

II

Reading the sky for signs. Years ago,
a ghost ship off Tor Bay — trailing
fire — ascended from water,
moved through veils of fog
above the wild roses.
What did it mean?

Someone would die. Today,
in an airplane over jewelled islands
of the South China Sea
a man held a trembling gun in one hand
(stuffing the passengers' money
into a drawstring bag with the other), kissed
a picture of the Virgin Mary
at the emergency
exit, where his partner pushed him
2,000 feet to his death: a fine example
of Newton's Second Law. The homemade
parachute didn't open. He slipped into damp earth
like a knife, only his fingertips showing,
new mushrooms in the soil.

III

Now strings of lights — red, orange,
green, yellow — are being turned out
all over the trailer park. A dog barks,
barks again. The stars shift,
unobserved. Each thing, moving,
tugs something else.

The child's mother carries her
back to the trailer. A thin moon is swinging
this way, that, in the sky. On either side
voices are wings. Something brushes
her cheek. You'll be fine, dear. The child knows
this, but likes to be carried. She can see
an eyebrow, an ear, a spangle of stars. Night's
breath. Where do we go
when we dream?
Her mother can't say. The trailer rocks slightly
as she opens the door, goes up the steps.

IV

Does love read the sky? Centuries ago,
Kepler arrived at a manor house
near Prague, shutting the coach door
with a smile. Life was bound to change
for the better. But he remained a guest
in someone else's house. As Tycho Brahe lay dying,
he tugged on the young man's sleeve:
Will they remember me? Will they know

my name?

Kepler could not say.
Student of the night sky, servant
of the mystical. Perhaps all of it
could be known by calculation. Think of him
walking across a bridge, over the Vltava —
after his wife and three children had died,
his mother accused as a witch — pausing
when a snowflake touched his sleeve. Six-sided
symmetry. Six known planets.
The number of reason, number of love. Surely
the universe folded and unfolded
every numbered thing.

V

Near the bridge in the trailer park,
a man sets up a tent, fumbling in the dark.
A woman unrolls the sleeping bag. They unzip,
shed themselves — a loosening shrug —
step inside each other. Breath:
fingering: blind:
quick. Body shudders,
stuns with its liquid, its cool —

they step back out. It's very still.
Breath after breath. One thing
draws another. Gently, so gently,
he puts his head against her ribs,
opening a shutter in her skin to look
inside: cathedrals of space, wandering
planets, aisle upon aisle
of stars. She summons all that's there.

VI

Who saw the burning ship in Tor Bay
years ago? A fisherman.
He was moving slowly —
water's vague surface
turned to air — in a dory,
oars drip, dripping, as he mapped shoals
in his mind. Ragged ends of fog
lifting like thought. Then the ship, a golden thing:
plumed bird. Devil. Hands shaking,
he put palms together. Whispering
the holy. *Sainte*. Knowing

what visions bring. *Priez pour nous.*
A fever. A drowning. Death's tooth,
sunk deep in the eye. What do we see
that might blind us? The ship,
a barque, passing over our heads,
unfolding the many hands
of mist. *Et á l'heure*. Drawing us
after it with veils of beauty, veils of fire.

VII

The girl is still awake. Where do we go
when we dream? Outside, a dog
keeps barking. And the moon, in a corner
of window: curve of eyelash.
Sometimes we drop
through the floor into nightmare. Falling,
falling, until the head hits something.
Another planet.

Another country.
A Russian physicist sits back, gazes
at his computer screen. Tears
in his eyes. He sees wonders:
each universe blown from another,
ours merely a soap bubble, clinging
to a cluster, one of many. Infinite universes
beyond time's loop, gravity's

laws. But here we are, earthed, each of us
with our hands up, fingertips showing
as we reach.

VIII

In the tent, the man kisses the woman.
Elbow, eyelash, ear. The symmetry
of details, things
that match. Breath: breath: breath:
lips to skin. Every kiss
an ellipse. How he loves her.

Each thing grips
space until it learns to curve. And space
clutches planets, stars,
teaching them

how to move. Hundreds of years ago
Galileo couldn't sleep. His crude telescope
magnified the white smudges:
Jupiter's moons. Unnamed, unnumbered.
And beyond,

all that happened
keeps happening: night's breath
unfolds into a woman holding a man
holding a woman.

Letting it go. Before Galileo,
Copernicus
set earth on its path,
put it in motion around the sun. His elegant
circles, one embracing another. A stone *plinks*
into water, leaving ripples.

Near the river, an elderly man walks,
a few stones in his closed hand, thinking
about his wife. Gone,
passed away. He's come back to this place
for nineteen years. All the way
from Nacogdoches, Texas. A life
of vinyl, high tensile electric or slick/barb wire
fencing. For three years, he's been alone.
Grief. More grief. He still has the green
indoor/outdoor carpet at the door, petunias
in a hanging basket. Now he smells wood smoke,
hears an ATV making one last
orbit around this side of the park, then

the other. He strolls. By the laundry,
a sign shows the distance to San Francisco.
Paris. Jerusalem. It starts
here, where coin dryers tumble
warm T-shirts and towels. Centre
of the moving world.

X

A world, a breath,
a thousand more. Someone
will die
believing this. Bruno's heresy
flickers: other worlds, other
gods. Licked by the same

heat: it explodes the heart,
blackens the skin. They burn him
in Campo dei Fiori, watch
his words go up
in smoke. Such faint
inscriptions, thin

whisperings. Who to believe?
The ghost ship — with flame-filled
sails, pennants of light
across Tor Bay —
glimpsed by those who trust
that fire might be air, and air
might be the thing that drowns us.

XI

Six pebbles slide
from the man's arthritic hand
into his pocket. The light in the Men's
illuminates stained toilets, cracked
cement floor. Pisses into the first bowl –
sour yellow arc – goes back outside.
The stones in his pocket
comfort him. Above, stars are miniature
thresholds, each one a Taj Mahal. Sleeping,
sleeping. In a trailer, a girl's arm
relaxes around a woolly animal,
its glass eye open,
always. It drops from the bed.

The old man saunters back to his Holiday
Rambler motorhome, opens the door
into forty-three feet of nothing
with its built-in solid cherry cabinets,
leather couches and full carousel hanging
unit in the main closet. Dark
matter between this
and that, deep in the Milky Way,
between galaxies, making itself
into an invisible Taj Mahal:
the one that isn't real,
but imagined. That grand mausoleum
of polished black, never built. Sorrow
that has no home.

XII

Tent of skin. Pegged

hard: breath: breath: breath:
a man's body deep
in a woman's, or
hers deep in his. She can't tell

breath
from breath. She sees
her own death and
his — even now —
sees how small they are

and large, so large, at the same
time. Light
years between
her fingertips. Heat
inventing and re-inventing them: blazing,
stretched, almost invisible, but

expanding

expanding

expanding

NOTES

"Little Stories" takes its inspiration from "The Franklin's Tale" in Geoffrey Chaucer's *The Canterbury Tales*.

"The Blue Hour" owes a debt to Constantine Cavafy's "The God Forsakes Antony." Cavafy's poem apparently refers to Plutarch's tale, based on the siege of Alexandria by Octavian. According to Plutarch, Antony heard Dionysus and his musical entourage passing through the city on the night prior to the siege, and realized that the god was abandoning him.

"Seven Paintings by Brueghel" is a corona written for Staten Island, New York. I am especially indebted to the photographer who took a series of aerial photographs of the WTC landfill site (*Cryptome*, January 25, 2002), which were subsequently posted on the Internet.

I am grateful to the Power Plant Contemporary Art Gallery in Toronto for having exhibited the innovative and surprising work of Tim Hawkinson in the summer of 2000. It was Hawkinson's *Wall Chart of World History from Earliest Times to the Present* (1997) that triggered the writing of "The Body Tattoo of World History."

John Wheeler, the eminent physicist, describes gravity in the following way: "Mass grips space by telling it how to curve; space grips mass by telling it how to move" (Interview with John Wheeler, January 27, 1998, in *The Elegant Universe* by Brian Greene). I took the liberty of reformulating his comment in "The Trailer Park" (VIII).

ACKNOWLEDGEMENTS

Some of these poems were first published in the following journals: *Descant,*
Grain, The Fiddlehead, and *The Malahat Review.* Several poems also appeared in
Coastlines: The Poetry of Atlantic Canada (Goose Lane, 2002) and in *Words Out*
There: Women Poets in Atlantic Canada (Roseway, 1999). "Little Stories" won the
Bliss Carman Poetry Award in 1999.

℘

"The Body Tattoo of World History" is dedicated to the memory of Yancy
Meyer's creative spirit. May it shine.

℘

I am grateful for the Canada Council grant that allowed me the time to write
many of these poems. I'm also thankful for havens such as the Leighton
Colony at the Banff Centre for the Arts. Some of these poems were written
at St. Peter's Abbey in Muenster, Saskatchewan, during the first colloquium
on *Nature Writing and Wilderness Thought.* The colloquium was sponsored by the
Centre for Rural Studies and Enrichment at St. Peter's College and facili-
tated by Tim Lilburn, Don McKay, and Jan Zwicky.

℘

Once again, a round of applause to Ellen Seligman, who keeps the poetry
door open at M&S, and to Anita Chong, whose hard work and patience is
much appreciated.

℘

Wild roses to Sue Sinclair for reading the manuscript with such generosity of spirit. An amaryllis to Jeanette Lynes, who also read these poems. To George and Gertrude Sanderson, a bouquet of wildflowers. Other writers — Marlene Cookshaw, Lynn Davies, Ross Leckie, and Jan Zwicky — offered excellent suggestions for individual poems. For the best tea and poetry talk, cheers to Pam MacLean. Many thanks, as well, to Dan Ahern, for doing the driving between Antigonish and Fredericton in 2002–03.

ಞ

Editors like Don McKay are rare; his attention to these poems has been keen as that of an owl. Special thanks to him for his gentle, witty, and intelligent assistance with this collection.

ಞ

Loving thanks to Jan and Jack Simpson, and to Jennifer and Sue for their wonderful support. As always, deepest thanks to Paul for his love and encouragement, and to David and Sarah for inspiration.